Pages 34 and 35:
Photo by
Harry V. Lacey.

© 1991
By T.F.H.
Publications,
Inc., Neptune,
N.J. 07753 USA

————— • —————

T.F.H.
Publications,
The Spinney,
Parklands,
Denmead,
Portsmouth
PO7 6AR
England

t.f.h.

Your First
CANARY

Sue-Rhee Pasca

Selection

The canary hobbyist, whether he is destined to become a full-fledged breeder and show participant or is content to keep a happy bird or two in a cage, requires a source of sound, accurate, and nontechnical information covering the major aspects of the hobby.

Although this book was designed to fill this purpose, it cannot substitute for the years of practical experience which the pet shop owner can offer to his customers, and it cannot be emphasized too strongly that such a relationship should be established from the beginning. Nothing, including this book, can take its place.

THE FIRST STEP

The first step in the initial purchase is, usually, to visit a pet shop and observe the various canaries. Naturally, you should choose a clean, well-run establishment with knowledgeable personnel. Talk to the owner or manager and get his opinion. The primary thing to expect from the seller is a written guarantee in respect to the bird's singing ability. Not infrequently, the selected bird has only recently arrived and is not yet acclimated to the new surroundings. However, once the bird is in your home, it can be expected to start singing within a week or two.

Remember that it is the male canary who sings. Since, to the amateur, most young canaries look alike, particularly before the first molt, the ability to sing is frequently used to determine the sex of the bird. (The female also makes an excellent subject because of her pleasant voice and her ready adaptability to training.) Because females do not sing, their prices are usually lower. The price of a male is determined both by his type and the quality of his song. The main step after the decision to buy, therefore, is to obtain a written guarantee stating that it is a male and will sing.

The next factors to consider are the general health of the bird; the cage and cage furnishings; and the type of bird to choose. Here is a brief checklist of signs of health to be closely watched for in the prospective pet: 1) A healthy canary is a lively canary. It is active in the cage and moves in an alert manner. 2) Even if the canary is not singing, it will at least be calling and chirping. If the canary is healthy, its appearance will be clean and lithe. 3) A sick bird is quiet and listless. Its feathers are puffed up and it sits on the perch almost continuously. 4) A canary with a cold shivers and sneezes. There is a slight watery discharge, and the droppings are white and watery. 5) If the canary has sore eyes, it may rub its head against the sides of the perch or the cage bars. The eyes will be inflamed and reddish. 6) Observe the general cleanliness of the installation where you intend to make your purchase and, in particular, the cleanliness of the prospective pet's cage.

WHAT TYPE?

The next point is to decide on the *type* of canary. Since, at this early stage, the basic idea is to make your first purchase and start to get practical experience, it would probably be best to select one of the more readily available kinds.

Here is a checklist of some of the kinds of canaries available today. Many other varieties, bred in the past, have died out because of lack of popularity. Others are no longer bred because they were not hardy enough.

Commercial Canary

Many of the more exotic breeds have died out simply because the general public was quite satisfied with the "commercial" canaries sold in most pet stores. The song of these birds is, in many cases, far superior to the song of the more exotic types which were originally bred for size and shape or color, rather than for voice.

The song of the standard canary is bright and cheerful, with crisp, bell tones blended with the notes common to the Roller canary. If a softer, roller-type song is preferred, it will be found that in any group of singers there is at least one bird with a softer tone. The clerk or manager should be consulted on this choice and, since the song will be guaranteed, his advice followed.

The size of the "commercials" is four or five inches. The color of the plumage is either bright yellow, yellow, yellow and green, or an occasional all-green singer who is a throwback to the first wild birds.

Red Factor

For many years, canary fanciers tried to develop a strain of red canaries. Many different wild birds with red plumage were mated with canaries but without success. Then approximately thirty years ago, the German breeder, Dr. Hans Duncker, discovered that a small South American bird, the Red-hooded Siskin, would mate with the canary.

Since that time, breeders have tried many combinations of these birds. However, it is only within the last decades that the strain has been perfected. These handsome newcomers can be found in all shades from very light orange or copper to a deep orange-red that is almost a pure red.

OTHER VARIETIES

There are many other varieties of canaries from which you can choose; each has its own particular appeal. The following are some of the better-known varieties: Border Fancy, Norwich, Yorkshire, Gloster Fancy, Lizard, Frill, Roller, Chopper, and Lancashire.

The canary is unrivalled when it comes to singing ability. In addition, it is a sturdy, attractive little bird that thrives in captivity. Photo by Michael Gilroy.

The canary was discovered by Spanish sailors more than 500 years ago in the Canary Islands, located off the northwest coast of Africa.

Care

At this early stage of the hobby, it is jumping the gun to go to such extremes as selecting an elaborate cage to blend in with the decor of the home. There are a great many kinds of cages available in many shapes and many colors. These vary anywhere from a foot or so square to two or three feet in length. The size and the degree of fashion are limited only by the amount of money one wishes to invest. It is best to be guided by the advice of pet shop personnel.

The amount of money required to purchase bird, cage, cage furnishings, and food is minimal. Here, too, the pet dealer can save the hobbyist a considerable amount of time by giving proper and knowledgeable advice. Basically, the dealer will say that you need the following: a cage equipped with perches; three or four food cups; bird gravel and gravel paper; cuttlebone; birdseed; and treat food. Now let's consider each of these in some detail.

PERCHES

The new pet needs several round or oval-shaped softwood perches in its cage. These should be of slightly different sizes so the feet don't get tired from always gripping in the same position. You may even wish to provide the canary with a flat perch an inch or more wide so that it may sometimes sit without having to cling at all.

Any new cage you purchase will be fitted with the necessary perches. Don't make the mistake of adding more perches so that the bird will have to fly through an obstacle course. Leave it a clear flyway so that it can get the necessary exercise. Also, check the perches periodically to make sure they are not loose and cannot turn when the canary alights.

OTHER FURNISHINGS

The cage should have one cup for food and another for water. One or two treat cups, fitted to the wires of the cage, should also be provided. These are for such treats and supplementary foods as song food, conditioning food, and fresh greens. A cuttlebone should be hung close to a perch and changed regularly. This not only keeps the beak in condition but also adds calcium to the diet. The floor of the cage should be covered with a thin layer of bird gravel. Gravel paper can also be used.

Any new cage will be painted or finished with materials that cannot harm your bird. If you decide to repaint an old cage, or alter the color of a new one, do not use a paint that has lead in it. Lead is as poisonous to birds as it is to humans. It is wise to avoid any oil paint. Use the latex types. Don't put your pet back into a freshly painted cage too soon. Also, it is best to keep your canary in a room well away from the odor of fresh paint whenever your home is being redecorated.

ACCLIMATION

Although canaries are highly domesticated, they are still capable of feeling ill at ease for the first few days in new surroundings. The pet has been subject to several changes in environment over a relatively short time and, therefore, requires a certain period in which to adjust. Until the canary shows signs of adjusting, do not expect it to sing. Permit the pet some privacy and see that it is well fed and warm.

When you first get the canary home, let it enter the cage by itself. Put the opened traveling box up to the open door of the cage and leave it there until it hops into the cage. If it has not gone into the cage voluntarily within an hour or so, pick it up gently and put it into the cage. The bird must be picked up gently. Hold it from above so that your hand covers the wings but leaves the feet free to move. Never grab a bird by the legs or tail or squeeze it to prevent struggling.

After your canary becomes accustomed to the new surroundings, it will greet you and your friends with a cheery song. As with humans, canaries like sunshine and a light room. But they cannot stand hot summer sun. Make sure

that no drafts reach the cage because chills are bad for birds and endanger their health. The cage should be covered from sunset to sunrise, particularly if strong artificial light is present. With insufficient sleep, the bird's health and singing ability can be adversely affected.

FEEDING

The canary fancier who decides to enlarge the scope of his hobby will eventually come to realize the immense importance of proper diet. However, the foundations of proper nutrition are basically the same for both the casual pet and the more specialized breeding varieties.

In general, the canary requires a balanced diet consisting, as does the human diet, of protein, carbohydrates, fats, vitamins, and minerals. The only difference between the balanced diet you feed your family and the balanced diet you feed your pet is the source of the various nutrients.

The canary's meals should consist mainly of a daily seed mixture, supplementary foods and treat foods, and plenty of fresh water. The best source of advice on the different brands and types of food for a canary is, again, your pet shop dealer.

SEED MIXTURE

A canary's chief food is seed. The daily seed mixture consists of seeds grown specifically for canaries and is known simply as canary seed. It is a long, narrow tan seed, pointed at

Yorkshire canary. This bird projects every outward appearance of good health and vitality.

In canary keeping, preventive health maintenance is easier to achieve than the cure of any particular disease or illness. Photo by Michael Gilroy.

each end. Mixed with the canary seed are rape seeds, a very nourishing seed that canaries like, and an assortment of other seeds in small amounts that give the bird different flavors and extra food values.

Give the canary fresh seed every day. It likes its food clean, fresh and sweet. Be sure that there is always seed in the cup. And that it is seed! Canaries husk the seeds before eating them, frequently dropping the husks back into the seed cup. This may give the cup the appearance of being full when it contains nothing of nutritive value. Blow gently on the mixture and the husks, which are lighter in weight, will blow away, leaving the seed.

SUPPLEMENTARY FOODS

Canary lovers have discovered that their pets appreciate and thrive on supplementary foods that help build resistance against sickness. Certain wild seeds are so appetizing that finding them in their cages from time to time acts as a signal for the canaries to start a song concert. The popular brands of bird foods provide such supplementary treats in the form of conditioning foods, song foods, molting foods, oat and groat mixtures.

Breeders have also discovered that eggs have value for canaries. A convenient way to provide the benefits of fresh egg is the commercially prepared egg-biscuit food that can be fed in conjunction with other supplementary foods. All

of the above can be given in the special treat cups previously described.

TREATS

Most canaries also relish certain treats such as biscuits or tidbits that are actually a mixture of different seeds cooked with honey. Other treats come in the form of little plastic cups which fit right on the cage, in which greens are grown or millet seeds are provided. Occasionally, a few well-washed greens can be given. The benefits of many varieties of fruit can be furnished in commercial mixtures that supply these fruits in dehydrated form, mixed with seeds.

In case you have never fed a canary before, here is a word of warning about treats. The treat items that you give your pet should be specially formulated for canaries. Delicacies such as cake from your table are entirely unsuitable. If your pet becomes fat and listless, it will stop singing. The best singers are the birds fed on proper canary food with the supplementary foods that are real "treats" for them.

CUTTLEBONE

Minerals and salts round out the canary's diet. It can get these from a piece of cuttlebone, which is the internal calcareous shell or bone of the cuttlefish. A piece of this bone should hang in the cage at all times, soft side in. By picking at it, the bird will keep its bill sharp, and the calcium in the cuttlebone will keep its bones strong and its beak hard. You will have to replace the cuttlebone about once a month.

WATER

Canaries love fresh water and they drink quite a bit. So be sure your pet is *never* left without it. During the summer months it is best to give fresh water twice a day. Of course, your pet will want to drink from a clean cup. Wash it daily so that it remains as clean as your own china.

GRIT

Bird grit or gravel plays an important part in feeding. Birds have no teeth; food is swallowed and stored in the crop. From there it enters the gizzard where the food is thoroughly ground up so that its nutritional values can be utilized. In order for the gizzard to do its work efficiently, the canary must eat a little grit or gravel. Keep an ample supply on the bottom of the cage where the bird can scratch around and pick up what it needs.

HOUSEKEEPING

Since cleanliness and sanitation are the fundamental preventives of disease, it is essential that the installation of a new pet in your home be accompanied with a program of proper canary housekeeping.

The program is an easy one, requiring only a few moments of routine effort. Following are some of the basic techniques recommended by authorities on canary-keeping.

Every other day the bottom of the cage should be cleaned out and a fresh layer of gravel supplied. This task is easier if gravel paper is used to line the cage bottom. Paper also saves your pet from having to walk on the metal cage floor. Use gravel in the cage—not sand or sawdust—because canaries must eat a certain amount of gravel in order to digest their food.

Clean the perches every time you clean the cage bottom. Do not wash them—the dampness can result in rheumatism—but scrape them with wire perch-scrapers available in pet shops.

Once a week, clean the cage thoroughly. Wash the walls and bars with a damp cloth or scrub them with soapy water. Then spray the cage with a mild disinfectant to keep away mites and other pests. Of course, during this kind of cleaning, you should put your pet in a spare cage. Make sure that the regular cage is thoroughly dry before returning the bird.

BATHS

If your canary has a clean home, he will do much to keep himself clean. He will spend hours preening his feathers to keep them clean and well arranged. As part of his plumage-care program, see that your pet gets regular baths. In summer, allow him the health-giving fun of a clean bath three or four times a week, if not every day. In winter, about once a week is enough, but

Manufacturers have made a wide range of canary foods available to today's fanciers. Some of the foods are especially useful for specific functions, such as song stimulators, color enhancers, conditioners, etc. Foods shown here are Living World foods from Rolf C. Hagen Corp.

Spray millet is one of the most popular of all canary treats/supplemental foods. The birds enjoy picking it from sprays hung in their cages.
Rolf C. Hagen Corp.

Perches should be cleaned thoroughly at least once a week.

make sure the room is warm.

You can buy a little canary bathtub that attaches to the side of the cage. Or you can put a little lukewarm water (about half an inch) in a shallow bowl on the bottom of the cage. Your pet will probably want to splash about and shake himself so much that he may leave a messy bath, just like a frisky youngster. Then you will have to clean and dry the cage. Never keep a canary in a damp cage. If your bird is hesitant about bathing, splash a little water on him when you set out the bath.

TOYS

Bird toys, such as a swing and a Ferris wheel, should be provided. A bird pacifier will act as an outlet for your pet's natural instinct to pull things, and thus can help to prevent harmful featherplucking.

HEALTH

Canaries are hardy birds who have lived so long in human society that man's dwelling has become their natural environment. If your canary is properly cared for, he will live a happy, contented life, filling your home with his cheery song. Your pet's resistance to disease always goes hand-in-hand with good care

and proper feeding. One of the best ways to avoid sickness in the canary is always to follow the rules for a well-balanced, nutritious diet.

Care is just as important as is proper diet. This involves regular housecleaning, including the cleaning of water and food cups, the bottom of the cage, perches, and the cage itself. Canaries should be kept out of drafts, and should never be left out in the bright sun.

A heartbreaking accident may occur if your canary escapes from its cage, unless you take care to prevent it. Mirrors are dangerous because a bird may fly directly into them. Household appliances can be threats to your pet's safety. Unscreened windows and outside doors should always be kept closed if there is any chance of your pet's escaping its cage.

AILMENTS

Although canaries are generally hardy, they can be subject to some illnesses and diseases. If your pet behaves in an abnormal fashion, it can be an indication that he is not well.

If you suspect a problem, contact your veterinarian regarding medical treatment.

Breeding

The most fascinating and creative aspect of canary-keeping is breeding. Breeding is the key to shows, and to social meetings with other canary fanciers. Most important of all, however, is the sense of creative achievement derived from this activity. Whether the beginner starts with one pair in a breeding cage or several pairs in a breeding aviary is immaterial—in either case both fun and possible profit are in the offing.

WHEN TO START

Many people believe that canary breeding should begin on Valentine's Day. Responsible pet shop experience suggests, however, that it is best to wait until March 1 or even March 25. This is especially true in particularly cold climates, even though your home is kept at an even temperature.

Probably the best canary for the beginning breeder is the Warbler. Warblers are hardy, all-around birds with beautiful plumage and a fine song. Let's assume that you have a fine male and want to buy him a mate. Your best bet is to depend on a reputable dealer to select a good female of unrelated stock. Because genes are inherited from both parents, as much care should be used in selecting a female as is used in choosing a male. An excellent

type male mated to a poor-quality female is not likely to produce top-quality babies. It goes without saying that both parents should be of the same variety; for example, Norwich to Norwich, Frill to Frill, etc.

The science of genetics is much too complex for a discussion here, but one point must be stressed. Colorful plumage is only one desirable characteristic. You also want fine singing, good carriage and, above all, healthy birds. Selecting mates on the basis of one trait only is not likely to pay off.

THE BREEDING CAGE

The next step after selecting the birds is to provide a breeding cage, which can be purchased in pet shops. The best size is approximately 24 x 24 x 12 inches. Ideally, the cage will have both a solid and a wire partition in the center.

Of course, provide the necessary seed and water cups and perches.

Next comes the nest. Metal nests are the easiest to clean and may be used over and over again. They can be bought from most pet shops. Do not hang the nest too high, as the parents will not be able to feed their youngsters. Remember, parent birds only feed their young when the young birds lift their heads and open their mouths. So they must be able to perch on the side of the nest with

Canary seed is the main staple of a canary's diet. Purchase only high-quality seed that is guaranteed to be fresh. Photo by Michael Gilroy.

To help ensure a successful canary breeding program, select only those birds that are hardy and sound.

their heads just above the mouths of the babies.

COURTSHIP

Now that you have bought your pair of canaries and have prepared a breeding cage, you can look forward to having additions to the canary family. Suppose, however, you put the two birds in the cage and they appear to dislike each other, or even worse, have a tendency to fight! Here is where the commercial breeding cage comes in handy. Leave both partitions in the center of the cage. Put the male in one section and the female in the other. After four or five days, take out the solid partition so that the birds can see each other. When they are ready to mate, you will hear their mating call, and the male will feed the female through the bars. Then you can remove the remaining partition. It is almost certain that mating will soon take place.

You will know when to give the female nesting material because she will start picking up feathers and any soft material she can find in the cage. At this time, provide *short* pieces of soft string or cotton, dried moss and grass, or even nesting hair. Caution: Do not put long pieces of string or long horsehairs in the cage. Your bird may use them for the nest and, sooner or later, the parents or young will get tangled up in them, perhaps fatally.

REMOVING THE EGGS

Replace each egg as it is laid with an artificial one, available from pet shops. Keep the eggs in a soft bed of absorbent cotton or soft cloth until the hen has laid her full number— from three to six. Then remove the artificial eggs and return the real ones to the nest, and let her begin to incubate them. This procedure ensures that all the eggs will hatch at the same time. It is best for both the mother and for the fledglings if the babies are all born on the same day. This ensures uniformity of size. Otherwise the first baby to hatch would be much older and larger by the time the last egg had hatched. Incubation takes about two weeks.

EGG-BINDING

A mother bird will, on occasion, become egg-bound. The usual cause is insufficient exercise or the wrong diet. Get your birds in tip-top condition before breeding and you won't have this worry. The symptoms of egg-binding make the problem easy to diagnose. The hen will sit with her feathers puffed up in obvious discomfort. Later, her eyes will seem even more drawn and strained, and she will sit huddled on the floor. If you find a hen in this condition, you must act quickly.

Heat and mineral oil are the prescribed treatment. Place a drop or two of mineral oil directly into the bird's beak and the same amount into the vent. Be careful not to insert the dropper too deeply or you may break the egg. Make sure the oil is down to the point of the dropper in order not to force air into the bird. The heat may be supplied in several ways. Probably the best way is to wrap a hot-water bottle in a towel and place the suffering hen on the towel. The heat should be over 100°F. This temperature is very warm to the hand. Remember, the normal temperature of a canary is about 108°F.

SHOULD YOU LEAVE THE MALE IN THE CAGE?

Canary breeders are not in complete agreement about whether to remove the male from the cage while the hen is incubating the eggs. If you want the male to sing, transfer him to a song cage nearby. Some males may not sing at all when they are with their mate in the breeding cage. If the male is young and without experience in nesting, he may annoy the hen. In that case, you should remove him from the cage and place him in a cage nearby. If you have only one pair, it is probably best to leave the male with the hen so he can help raise the youngsters, if he seems to be helping rather than annoying her.

FEEDING YOUNG BIRDS

You do not have to do any of the work in feeding the young birds because the parents take care of it themselves. You should provide egg-biscuit food and nestling food so that the parent birds will have suitable and nutritious food with which to feed their babies. Young birds are voracious eaters and require feeding at very frequent intervals throughout the day. Make sure that the special food you furnish for the youngsters is on hand at all times. This food is readily available at pet shops.

Occasionally, parent birds neglect to feed their young. This usually happens when both parents are young birds raising their first family. For this reason, it is wise to have at least one parent about two years old, preferably the female. This is a good point to remember when you are selecting a mate for your first canary and plan to breed them for the first time. Your pet shop probably can sell you a hen who has raised at least one family. If the parents do not feed the young birds, the parent birds should be removed from the cage. You will have to take over the task by hand-feeding.

Moisten a combination of nestling food and egg-biscuit food and feed the baby birds from a small spatula. You probably won't have any difficulty in getting the babies to eat because the slightest movement over their nest will get them to open their mouths when they need food. Canaries, like most other songbirds, can raise several families in the breeding season. One of the problems for the beginning breeder is knowing when to remove the young from the first nest and knowing when to stop the breeding. Young birds can be taken away from their parents when they are five or six weeks old. Continue to feed the egg-biscuit food and nestling food,

Before you begin canary breeding, you should be fully familiar with the biology of these birds.

Canaries are generally hardy little birds that are relatively undemanding in their maintenance needs. Photo by Michael Gilroy.

but also start to provide regular canary-seed mixture. Young birds often have trouble in handling hard seeds at first and may need some soft food for a time. For raising young canaries, many pet experts recommend egg food or egg-biscuit food along with the nestling food. Remember, however, that hard seeds are the canary's natural food, and they should gradually be weaned to a seed diet. If they have trouble cracking the seeds, you can do it for them with a rolling pin—crack, don't crush.

THE LAST NEST

The question of when to allow the last nest is also of importance. Some beginners are so enthusiastic about the fine youngsters their pets are raising that they let the parents breed as long as they want to nest. When the birds are paired early, they could have three nests by the first of July. If the birds seem strong and healthy, the beginner is likely to permit one more nest. However, it is recommended that only one "clutch" or set of eggs be permitted the first year. With more experience, you can then decide whether the birds can stand the rigors of a second or third clutch the following year.

Experience—with success, as well as a few disappointments —is the only way to learn how to breed canaries successfully. Perhaps the biggest mistake any beginner can make is to become too interested, too attentive toward his birds.

Remember, birds want privacy in which to carry out their parental functions. Don't show off the nest, the first egg, the nestlings to every visitor. Give your pets a proper diet and privacy and they will do all the work. Provide help only when they need it.

MOLTING

Most birds, canaries among them, enter into molt immediately after breeding. They should not be permitted to breed right up to the time they start molting. Molting, however, is a perfectly normal condition and one that a healthy bird can go through with ease. It is not a good idea for them to molt while still raising their last brood. Give them a rest between the duties of a parent and the task of renewing their beautiful plumage for the coming year.

Warm climates trigger the molting season, causing it to begin earlier and to finish earlier. Cool climates delay the molt, causing it to last longer. In most areas, the molt will be completed in about six weeks. The usual regular care, keeping cages meticulously clean, and keeping the birds out of drafts will usually see them through the molt without problem. A commercially prepared molting food should be fed at this time to ensure a proper diet. Loss of feathers to such an extent that the canary shows bald spots or loses its ability to fly is abnormal and should be looked into. It may be because of poor diet, parasites, or improper environment.

SHOW TIME

Many canary owners become so fascinated with these birds that they begin to breed canaries as a hobby. Once they have turned into really serious breeders, it is only a short step before they want to raise specimens for show and exhibit the outstanding canaries from their breeding cages. Raising and training show canaries is an exacting but rewarding task.

For a beginning breeder, the first step toward learning all about your new hobby is to attend canary shows and to consult with the keeper of your favorite pet shop. At the shows you can learn about the many varieties of canaries and see them on the show bench. You will learn to tell the difference between a fine bird that is still only a beautiful pet and the show bird that wins prizes.

Probably the best way to get started is to become a member of an active bird club. Experienced club members are always willing to share their knowledge with new members. You can avoid many mistakes by accepting the advice that only an old hand can give.

Remember, a show specimen must be much more than a bird in perfect color and good health. A bird is judged on many other factors, including size, depth of color, contour, position, etc. Particular attention is given to the bird's head, neck, shoulders, wings, etc. In addition to having a near-perfect bird, the exhibitor must train his birds so they do not flutter nervously or refuse to move correctly.

Your best canary may behave perfectly in the breeding rooms; it may accept the show cage readily. However, when you take it to its first formal show, the bird may flutter or fail to move promptly. If this should happen, the judge will refuse to consider the entry despite its other merits.

The solution to making show birds behave correctly is to train them carefully so you will be assured that they will be at their best when shown. First of all, they must become accustomed to the show cage by being frequently run into it. A small training stick about a foot long should be used to direct them in movement from their regular cage into the show cage. Use this stick often so that when they see it they will know that you want them to move.

Show birds must learn to become accustomed to strangers and be willing to let them handle the show cage. So while you are training your pets, ask visitors to quietly handle their cages. In time, even nervous birds will learn to accept strangers.

As soon as you are convinced that you have birds capable of being shown, you should start their training. Since shows are usually held in the early fall when canaries are in their finest plumage, you will want to have your birds well trained before the announced date. Once you are sure your birds are well trained, you can reduce the training time, but continue to use the show

A Frill canary. Canaries come in a multitude of varieties and beautiful colors. Photo by Michael Gilroy.

Young Gloster Fancy canaries. For some hobbyists, nothing beats the satisfaction of raising a canary family.

cage throughout the show season.

GROOMING

All birds groom themselves and keep their feathers in top condition. Wild birds, whose very life depends on the condition of their plumage, spend hours every day in preening their feathers. This means that you do not have to worry too much about the bird's appearance because he will attend to it very well himself. In the first months after molting, a canary is at its best and will require little care. As the season wears on, however, the plumage may begin to show the effects of dirt and soot. Owners living in large industrial cities will be distressed to find their birds becoming dingier and dingier. In this situation, the only solution is to wash the birds.

Washing is a necessary evil in a sense, since it is exhausting for the canary. Frequent washing, also, will affect the color and appearance of the plumage. It does, however, have to be done occasionally.

The best way to learn how to wash a bird is to have an experienced club member or your pet shop dealer demonstrate the procedure. The important points to remember are that the bird should be washed gently, rinsed thoroughly, and dried carefully. The procedure should be carried out in a warm room absolutely free of drafts with a drying cage kept very warm until the bird is thoroughly dry.

Crooked and twisted feathers can usually be straightened by using warm water. Crests may sometimes lie raggedly after a wash and must be arranged into position.

In general, you will have to depend on careful breeding, good care, proper diet, and the birds themselves, in order to produce acceptable show specimens.

RECORD KEEPING

Keeping complete and accurate records is of vital importance to a breeder in any field. These records permit proper pairing and prevent matings that would weaken the stock. In a sense, these records are pedigrees.

Records can be simple, but they should at least include the following information: the good and bad points of each bird; the date of mating; the number of eggs laid; the number of birds hatched; the number of birds raised.

Some of this information may appear unnecessary; however, it is useful in improving the stock. Neglectful parents or bad feeders and birds that seldom produce a goodly number of young birds must be weeded out of the breeding stock.

Once a sound breeding stock is established, the records will help the breeder to continue producing fine birds. They will let you advise others on how to pair birds they may purchase from you. When you want to buy additional birds, good records can assure you that your new birds are of unrelated stock and of the type you need.

In General

In earlier chapters we considered some of the basics of canary-keeping on a simplified "how-to-do-it" approach. One thing must, by now, have become apparent to the reader: keeping a canary is a threshold to a much wider application of what has, for years, been one of the world's most fascinating hobbies.

Due to the concise nature of this text, it is not possible to explore, in depth, each category of interest related to canary-keeping. However, in the general sense, we can still discuss in further detail some of the more important areas. It should be remembered, however, that the real sources of information for the advanced canary fancier are the keepers of shops specializing in these birds, the various breeding and show societies, and the books written by the top authorities in the field.

TRAINING

Requiring a degree of patience not too often found, this activity reflects well on the talent, creativity, and self-discipline of the novice breeder. Training of the bird should begin at an early age: when it is about four weeks old. At that time, a show cage should be hung in the home aviary and the young bird introduced to it so that it will become used to being on display and attracting public attention. It is wise to let visitors gently handle the bird (under supervision) so that natural habits of relaxation will be formed. Remember that the training stick should be used *gently* as a guide toward proper movement, not as an instrument of compulsion. Use it to induce the young birds to run into the show cage frequently so they may be managed easily when the real competition starts. In about two weeks, the young birds should be conditioned to the show cage and emphasis on position training can then begin. Following are some general guidelines of training which make for excellent home shows, while still forming a sound foundation for competition training: 1) Start the

The Norwich canary, one of the larger varieties of canary, is well-rounded and chubby in appearance.

A natural perch can be offered to your canary, but be certain that it has not been chemically treated. Photo by Michael Gilroy.

When selecting your canary, look for a bird that is in good condition: bright-eyed, alert, and well groomed. Photo by Michael Gilroy.

training early, while the bird is still a nestling. 2) Finger train it first, then teach it more advanced tricks. 3) A trained canary requires more food than does an untrained one. Use the treat-reward system to inspire it and keep it up to a high standard. 4) Birds are extremely sensitive and go into shock easily. Therefore, never frighten the bird by losing your temper. 5) Start your training in trios and pairs of birds so they will be company for each other.

Once you have accustomed your birds to finger perching, obtain a small perching bar eight to ten inches long and, working seated at a small table, bring the bar gently across the birds' chests so they will hop onto it. Then reverse the procedure so they will hop from bar to finger. The second stage is to place the bar slightly higher than their beaks so they will fly to it and then back to the finger.

The following rules must be strictly adhered to: 1) Never force a bird through an act; it if refuses, put it back in the cage and resume training the next day. 2) Always reward the canary with a treat afterwards.

Finally, keep in mind that a tired bird cannot learn. Don't set too high a standard.

SHOW TIPS

One of the problems confronting the new canary hobbyist who seeks to enter the show world is the tendency to aim too high. It is usually wiser for the novice breeder to enter the less competitive local shows until he has acquired a fine polish of experience.

One of the best reasons for initial concentration on local events lies in the difficulty inherent in packing and shipping canaries to distant shows. Transportation agents cannot always be relied upon to feed and water the birds, and sometimes the pets are left for hours in exposed areas or placed next to cats or dogs. The result is a sick or upset bird unfit for show competition.

Be sure to visit a canary exhibition before attempting to compete in one. While luck is a vital, undeniable factor in any competition, the smart fancier leaves as little to chance and the whims of serendipity as possible. Proper training of your choicest specimen, an impeccably presented show cage, and passable knowledge of competition etiquette and the breed standard help ensure your bird's equable chance to make "specials," "Best Hen" or "Best Novice," or even a class First!

If birds must be shipped to distant shows, an over-ration of seed and water should be placed in the box or cage. Not too infrequently the show-orientated hobbyist will find himself in a position where he may be asked to take part in the management of a show. The roles here are many and varied, ranging anywhere from stewardship and public relations to actual judging and secretarial work.

Show personnel should be selected as many months in advance as possible. A good show is the result of good teamwork and the sooner the members of the team start working together the better the show will be.

LIFESPAN

It is of interest to note that female canaries, owing to the loss of vitality during the breeding season, may not live more than five or six years. However, there are some canaries, apparently males, who have been known to reach the ripe old age of sixteen years. One expert reports knowing of one that was twenty years old and still active.

VACATION CARE

One of the most important things that a canary-fancier who plans on taking a vacation or business trip can do is to place his pet in the care of a pet shop that furnishes boarding service.

There the pet will receive experienced care and will not be subject to possible accidents or improper care by an inexperienced friend or neighbor.

SUMMER CARE

Canaries, generally, should be kept in a room temperature of approximately 70°F and should be fed once daily. During excessively hot weather, give the bird fresh, cool water several times a day. Above all, keep the pet away from air conditioners and drafts. Both are harmful to canaries.

Bibliography

ALL ABOUT CANARIES
by Irene Evans
ISBN 0-87666-753-1
PS315
Audience: With adequate detail for the beginning canary owner, this book covers important areas of interest including metabolism, preening, housing, feeding, handling, training, breeding and exhibiting. The text also touches on the desirability of birds in one's home and the origin and history of the canary.
Hardcover, 5½ x 8", 96 pages, illustrations in color and black/white.

CANARIES AND RELATED BIRDS
by Horst Bielfeld
ISBN 0-86622-646-X
H-1089
Audience: An important volume in any canary library, Bielfeld's volume comprises two masterful works on finches, covering the canary and its close avian cousins. In-depth information, laced with color illustrations, makes this book incomparable for the fancier.
Hardcover, 6 x 9", over 200 full-color photographs.

ENCYCLOPEDIA OF CANARIES
By G.T.Dodwell
ISBN 0-87666-952-6
H-967
Audience: This lavishly illustrated reference book has proven indispensable to every newcomer to the fancy, as well as seasoned canary folk. Its coverage includes the many varieties available in Europe and North America, plus breeding theory, management, health care and exhibition. These and other areas covered in substantial, easy-to-understand detail. A must for all serious keepers.
Hardcover, 5½ x 8", 288 pages, fully color-illustrated.